ONESIMPLEWORD

HOW TO HAVE LIFE-CHANGING CONVERSATIONS

ONE SIMPLE WORD

HOW TO HAVE LIFE-CHANGING CONVERSATIONS

Todd A. Sinelli

LIT TORCH PUBLISHING

www.littorch.com

ONESIMPLEWORD
By Todd A. Sinelli

Published by

LIT TORCH PUBLISHING

8624 W. Catherine
Chicago, IL 60656
www.littorch.com

Library of Congress Cataloging-in-Publication Data

Sinelli, Todd A.
One Simple Word / Todd A. Sinelli.
p. cm.
ISBN 978-1-887357-04-3
1. Christian life. I. Title.
BV4501.3.S5843 2009
248.4--dc22
2009007202

Designed by Julie Curtis Design
Printed in the United States of America.
First edition, 2009

1 2 3 4 5 6 7 — 15 14 13 12 11 10 09

The questions we ask and the questions we answer can profoundly impact our lives.

Also by Todd A. Sinelli

One Lit Torch

True Riches

CONTENTS

INTRODUCTION

May I Ask You a Question?

Have you ever thought about what a question can do? A simple question contains the power to profoundly impact your life, both positively and negatively. I was fourteen when I first learned this truth.

Of all the questions I've ever been asked, the one that stands out the most was by my high school basketball coach. I was a freshman playing in an inner-squad scrimmage. I had just stolen the ball. I turned quickly and scored on the nearest basket. Mistakenly, this was my team's basket. The coach blew the whistle and shouted, "Sinelli, are you stupid?"

I did not think so at the time, but perhaps I was? I had no answer. I guess it was stupid to score on my own basket. Shouting this question amidst my friends and teammates really belittled me. I felt horrible. After that day, I no longer had a desire to play basketball. Nor did I have the desire to be around this coach.

Thomas Merton once said, "A person is known better by his questions than his answers." I will always remember my high school basketball coach by his question. And as I have had time to reflect, I am glad he asked. Soon afterward, I switched to lacrosse and earned first team All-State, All-Midwest, and All-Academic awards. Those successes would not have happened had it not been for that one impactful question.

Questions, to this day, intrigue me. Over the years I have made a habit of asking people, "What questions have impacted your life the most?" One 82-year-old man recounted how 36 years ago he was asked, "Would you like to go to a meeting?" The meeting was Alcoholics Anonymous. His life changed after answering "yes" and has been sober ever since. For one 29-year-old woman the life-changing question was, "Will you marry me?" Three kids and seven years of wedded bliss later, she is delighted she answered, "yes." Another person said the most impactful question in his life was, "Do you wanna take a hit?" He regrets not saying, "No" and got caught up in a life of drugs.

Many of us like to have the right answer when asked a question. We want to say the right thing at the right time. However, very few people actually do say the right thing at the right time. A friend of mine once asked a woman how long she had been pregnant. She was not. He later said, "*Never*, ever, ever ask a woman if she is pregnant. Always have her tell you. Make this mistake once and you will never forget it!" Saying the wrong thing at the wrong time is awkward. Yet, even an awkward question can be a pivot point in our lives. That woman went on to lose weight and get in great shape.

What else can a question do? A question can begin a relationship. Think about the people you know. Most of your relationships probably began with a simple question like, "What is your name?" or "How are you doing?" Questions allow us to interact with one another and they also act as a barometer for the depth of the relationship. Asking someone, "Would you like to join me for coffee?" is far different than, "Will you marry me?"

Jesus Christ, God incarnate, is the only One who always said the right thing at the right time. He was the Master of Masters in regard to asking and answering questions. His questions challenged, confronted and changed lives. His answers stunned some, sobered others and soothed many.

Where is your faith?
What do you wish?
What are you looking for?
Does this shock you?
Who do you say I am?
Why do you call me Lord and not do what I say?

Theologian John Dear found 307 questions that Jesus asked throughout the Gospels.[1] What is the reason for so many questions? Most of us would have preferred answers. Christian apologist Ravi Zacharias said, "Jesus Christ in the New Testament nine times out of ten when somebody asks Him a question replies with another question because a question does two things. Number one, it forces the questioner to open up within his own assumptions. Number two, it determines the entry point of a discussion."[2]

Jesus interacted with men, women, kings, kids, soldiers and prostitutes. He came with answers. He came with Truth. And He came with questions. In the Bible we are only given a glimpse into about 45 days of Jesus' life.[3]

Some two thousand years later, we are still challenged by His words, His actions and more specifically, by His questions.

One Simple Word

Jesus provided a word—one simple word—that can profoundly impact your life. This one word can bring excitement into your life, lift you out of depression, deepen your relationship with friends, family, and even with God. This one simple word can determine what you'll have for dinner, who you will marry, and possibly where you will spend eternity.

Sound too good to be true? The Bible says, "Test everything. Hold on to the good" (1 Thes. 5:21). So, test this one simple word. Test this idea. Test this pattern Jesus modeled throughout His life.

The one simple word I want to share with you is from the teaching Jesus gave during the Sermon on the Mount in Matthew 7:7. It is here that Jesus gives us a command, a direction, and this one simple word—**ask**.

Ask. One simple word with tremendous power.

In the pages ahead, we will explore how questions are asked and used in the Bible. Some of these questions you may have never noticed before, others will be very familiar. For example, would you happen to know Jesus' most frequently asked question? How about the first question ever asked? Would you like to learn the one question to avoid in your relationship with God and others? Do you know the one biblical question everyone must answer? If not, keep reading. This one simple word will help you enjoy relationships at their best and teach you the profound impact a question can have.

Let's begin with Jesus' most frequently asked question—do you know what it is?

CHAPTER ONE

Jesus' Most Frequently Asked Question

In 1965, John Lennon from The Beatles wrote a song titled "Help". The lyrics are:

Help! I need somebody.
Help! Not just anybody.
Help! You know I need someone.
Help! Won't you please, please help me?

John Lennon said he wrote the song in a state of confusion and depression while The Beatles grew more and more successful each day. He felt miserable and turned to alcohol despite immense fame and fortune. Not withstanding the fact that he had all the things money could buy, could afford the world's best physicians, could purchase the nicest homes and could travel wherever he desired, Lennon needed help. He asked for help, sang about help, and looked for it everywhere. Yet, what kind of help was he looking for and from whom?

The truth is that we all need help. But where will we find it? Is it waiting for us in alcohol, anti-depressants or self-help books? Who should we turn to when we wrestle with spiritual or relationship issues? Mom? Dad? Maybe a best friend? Or is there actually help to be found in God and the counsel we receive from His Scriptures?

Jesus asked a lot of questions in the Bible. Would you happen to know the question He asked most frequently? With this question, He positioned Himself as the greatest helper this world has ever seen. You may be surprised to learn the question is, "What do you want me to do for you?"

Jesus asked this question to those following Him (John 1:38), to His disciples (Mark 10:36), to the blind (Matt 20:32, Luke 18:41) and I believe He is asking every one of us today, "What do you want me to do for you?"

Consider for a moment who is asking this question. It is not your neighbor, doctor or favorite uncle. It is Jesus, the King of Kings and Lord of Lords. He is God Almighty, the Creator of all.

He is enduringly strong. He is entirely sincere. He's immortally graceful. He's imperially powerful. . . His goodness is limitless. His mercy is everlasting. His love never changes. His Word is enough. His grace is sufficient. His reign is righteous. His yoke is easy and His burden is light. . . He's incomprehensible, He's invincible, and He is irresistible.[4]

Jesus is all knowing. He is familiar with all your ways. He knows when you sit and when you rise. He knows every word you are about to say before it is on your tongue (Ps. 139). He knows every hair on your head (Matt. 10:29-31). He is your greatest encourager (2 Thes. 2:16-17). He is your greatest comforter (2 Cor. 1:3-7). And He can help "immeasurably more than all we ask or imagine, according to His power that is at work within us" (Eph. 3:20). He is God. He can do anything. Shouldn't He be the first One we turn to for help?

Where we look for help often determines what help we will find. The Psalmist writes, "Where does my help come from? My help comes from the Lord, the Maker of heaven and earth" (Psalm 121:1-2). The author of Hebrews tells us God has said, "Never will I leave you; never will I forsake you." So we say with confidence, "The Lord is my helper; I will not be afraid" (Heb. 13:5-6).

In his book *Questions of Jesus*, John Dear writes, "In Jesus, we have a God who is humble, loving, and generous, a God who longs to serve humanity, especially in its brokenness, poverty, and blindness. Jesus said He came 'not to be served but to serve.' With this question, we see once more how serious He is."[5] He continues, "The most frequently asked of Jesus' questions is also the most beautiful: 'What do you want me to do for you?'"

What do you *really* want Jesus to do for you? What is the reason you follow Him? What type of help are you looking for from Him? Stop for a moment and ponder His most frequently asked question.

What do you want Me to do for you?

I used to constantly ask God to make me rich. Now, I ask Him to make me wise. My story is this. I was broke at age 24. A millionaire at 25. A multi-millionaire at 26. Nearly broke again at 28. I have been a trader in the financial markets and have literally made and lost millions of dollars in this profession. Over the years, I have found three things to be true:

1. When I had much I wanted more.
2. The things I bought only satisfied for a short time.
3. Being without has always deepened and developed my knowledge and understanding of God in ways that money never could.

At 25, I had over a million dollars in the bank, an Italian wardrobe, a Mercedes and a Range Rover. Then I decided to buy a Ferrari. What came next was one of the most disappointing experiences of my life.

I traveled to Florida to purchase a Ferrari 328 gtsi from a heart surgeon who lived next door to the famous wrestler Hulk Hogan. I pulled up to his multi-million dollar mansion ready to acquire this car as a trophy symbolizing my financial success. I expected the car to be faster than any other vehicle I had ever driven. I expected the seats to be soft and sensuous as I sat in them. I wanted this car to affirm how good life could be by owning the best of the best. However, when I got into the car the seats were stiff, hard and rather uncomfortable. But that did not matter because I knew once I hit the accelerator it would rocket me to the back of my seat. Surprisingly, the car was no faster than a Ford Mustang GT. It did not throw me back and it accelerated much slower than expected. I thought, *Is this as good as it gets? Really, is this the best life has to offer?* I did not buy the car and I sadly realized that I was seeking fulfillment from the things in this world more than I was seeking fulfillment in my relationship with God.

Jesus is the One who "will meet all your needs according to his glorious riches in Christ Jesus" (Phil. 4:19). It is in His power to give us whatever He chooses. As a loving father instructs his child, as a master teaches an apprentice, as a Rabbi directs his disciples, Jesus tells us that the meaning of life and the purpose of existence is found in a deep personal relationship with Him (John 10:10), not the things of this world (1 John 2:17). For us to understand this, we must grasp that spiritual life is of greater value than any physical possession.

God can give us anything. We know this. So what should the things we ask for be? Cars? Clothes? Cash? Sometimes He does give us these things; other times, He does not. However, a relationship with Him should be what we want more than anything else.

A confederate soldier noted how God answered his prayers:

I asked God for strength, that I may achieve;
I was made weak, that I might learn humbly to obey,
I asked for health, that I might do greater things;
I was given infirmity, that I might do better things.
I asked for riches, that I might be happy;
I was given poverty, that I might be wise.
I asked for power, that I might have the praise of men;
I was given weakness, that I might feel the need of God.
I asked for all things; that I might enjoy life;
I was given life, that I might enjoy all things.
I got nothing that I asked for, but everything that I had hoped for.
Almost despite myself, my unspoken prayers were answered.
I am, among all men, most richly blessed.

Please don't misunderstand me; there is nothing wrong with having a lot of things or asking God for lots of money. When I see people making large amounts of money, my immediate prayer is for them to enjoy it and to use it wisely. There are countless examples in Scripture of very wealthy and very godly people ranging from Father Abraham who had his own standing army to Joseph of Arimathea who purchased fine linen for the body of Jesus and donated the tomb. Barnabas was a wealthy landowner who used his wealth to help start the early church, bless the poor and support missionaries. Money can be a wonderful resource in our lives; however, it should not be what we desire most from God.

Many of us have been conditioned to think money is a sort of panacea to our problems. We think, *If I only had more money, many of my problems would be solved.* Perhaps this is partially true. I imagine close to 90% of your problems could be solved with money. Your rent, overdue bills, taxes, and things like car repairs can be solved with money. However, the really interesting problems in life are the ones that money cannot solve: a failing marriage, a terminal disease, reconciling a difficult relationship, sorrow from the loss of a loved one and your eternal destination. The Bible offers hope and solutions to all these topics and to all the "interesting problems" to which money offers no solution. 2 Peter 1:3-4 says, "His divine power has given us everything we need for life and godliness through our knowledge of him who called us by his own glory and goodness. Through these he has given us his very great and precious promises, so that through them you may participate in the divine nature and escape the corruption in the world caused by evil desires."

The evidence is all around us. Many financially successful people have publicly declared that money and possessions are not the keys to happiness. Yet, few of us seem to believe their words. Pasi Falk writes in *Hitting the Jackpot: Lives of Lotto Millionaires* that after someone has all the things that money can buy, what they then want are things money cannot buy. Health, happiness, friends and family that love them, peace of mind and peace in their household were their primary desires. Money could not purchase the things they longed for most.

Actor Brad Pitt was interviewed in Rolling Stone magazine:

Pitt: Man, I know all these things are supposed to seem important to us—the car, the condo, our version of success—but if that's the case, why is the general feeling out there reflecting more impotence and isolation and desperation and loneliness? If you ask me, I say toss all this—we gotta find something else. Because all I know is that at this point in time, we are heading for a dead end, a numbing of the soul, a complete atrophy of the spiritual being. And I don't want that.
Rolling Stone: So if we're heading toward this kind of existential dead end in society, what do you think should happen? **Pitt:** Hey, man, I don't have those answers yet. The emphasis now is on success and personal gain. I'm sitting in it, and I'm telling you, that's not it. I'm the guy who's got everything. I know. But I'm telling you, once you've got everything, then you're just left with yourself. I've said it before and I'll say it again: it doesn't help you sleep any better, and you don't wake up any better because of it.[6]

What Brad Pitt and lottery millionaires are missing is the truth from Jesus' words that "a man's life does not consist in the abundance of his possessions" (Luke 12:15). True life exists in knowing God and seeking Him first while enjoying contentment with a lot or a little. The Bible teaches, "godliness with contentment is great gain. For we brought nothing into the world, and we can take nothing out of it"(1 Tim. 6:6-7). Pastor John Piper frequently remarks, "God is most glorified in us when we are most satisfied in Him." When we have good health, thank the Lord. When He provides financially, thank Him. When He provides a spouse, great friend, or new car, thank Him. Even when He doesn't give us certain things, we should thank Him for it is God's will to give thanks in all circumstances (1 Thes. 5:18).

Our financial status may change. Our health can change. But God never changes. "Jesus Christ is the same yesterday and today and forever" (Heb. 13:8). Although God never changes, we, surprisingly, do through a relationship with Him. It is astonishing how quickly we take on the characteristics of those we are constantly around.

In the Gospel of Mark, we learn the disciples, James and John, came to Jesus with an incorrect understanding of how to be great. They said, "Teacher, we want you to do for us whatever we ask." Jesus asks, "What do you want me to do for you?" They respond by saying they wanted the position of sitting on his right and on his left when He comes to power. Jesus tells them, "You don't know what you are asking" (Mark 10:38) and then calls the other ten disciples together to teach them that, "whoever wants to become great among you must be your servant . . . for even the Son of Man did not come to be served, but to serve, and to give his life as a ransom for many." Jesus corrected their selfish requests and teaches them that a great life exists in being a great servant.

Studying Jesus, we see how He took on the very nature of a servant, giving us an example of how to serve and become great in God's eyes.

Learning to serve is God's path for us toward greatness. This principle applies to our relationships with God, one another and even those in business. In 1982 the restaurant chain Chick-fil-A was going through some tough times. They held an executive meeting and asked, "Why do we exist?" Their answer birthed a corporate purpose statement that included, to "glorify God by being a faithful steward of all that's entrusted to us and to have a positive influence on all who come in contact with Chick-fil-A."[7]

After a customer places an order the staff is trained to respond by saying, "It is my pleasure." They do not say, "You are welcome" or "Please come again." They say, "It is my pleasure." Taking pleasure in serving others is a foundational principle in the Chick-fil-A business plan. This is also a foundational principle in being a follower of Jesus Christ.

What if we answered Jesus' most frequently asked question by responding, "Lord, teach me to be a great servant"? How would our lives change? What would it look like if we embraced Jesus' example, "Who, being in the very nature God, did not consider equality with God something to be grasped, but made Himself nothing, taking the very nature of a servant"? (Phil. 2:6-7)

Take a moment and think about how are you becoming more like Jesus. Who are the people you are serving? What questions do you find yourself asking the most? There are over 300 questions by Jesus recorded in the Bible; how many can you recall?

Most Christians I have spoken with cannot recall one, let alone three of Jesus' questions. One of the reasons I wrote this book is to remind people to answer God's questions. There is a joy and inner peace found in conversing with the Lord. Many of us are so busy bombarding Him with our questions that we never answer His.

Answer Jesus' most frequently asked question.

What do you want me to do for you?

What is your answer? _____

This question invites us to be honest with God and to seek the rich spiritual relationship He offers above all things. Jesus' question also compels us to re-consider what we want. A recent study by The Barna Group found that the top desires among adults in the United States were:

1. Physical health
2. Living with integrity
3. One marriage partner for life
4. A clear purpose for living
5. A close relationship with God[8]

The Bible directs us to pray for health, integrity, a spouse, purpose and a close relationship with the Lord.

1. For physical health: 3 John 2
2. For living with integrity: Prov. 11:3, 22:1, Titus 2:7
3. For a marriage partner: Prov. 19:14, 20:6, 31:10
4. For living with a clear purpose: Rom. 8:28-29, 12:1-2, 1 Cor. 10:31, Col. 2:2-3
5. For a close relationship with God: Matt. 6:33, 11:28-30, 22:36-40, Eph. 5:1-2, James 4:8, 2 Peter 1:2-11

However, I challenge you to make your relationship with God your number one prayer. May your heart's desire be to know Christ (Phil. 3:10), to grow in the grace and knowledge of Jesus (2 Peter 3:18), and to become more like God by looking to serve instead of being served (Matt. 20:28).

May your most frequently asked question soon become, "What would you like me to do for you?" and your favorite response be, "It is my pleasure" as you meet numerous opportunities to help those who are pleading, "Help, I need somebody. Help, not just anybody. Won't you please, please help me?"

One simple word, **ask**. Ask God to help you become great in His eyes. Ask to become a great servant. Ask to be like Jesus.

Take some time and think about the people in your life. Do they see you as a servant or as one constantly looking to be served? Do you know what areas in life they could use help? Have you asked them? What habits can you work on in the days ahead to be more Christ-like?

Take a deep breath, smile and exhale. Think about Jesus. As the greatest servant who ever walked among us, may we follow His unprecedented example and experience abundant life by becoming more like Him through the questions we ask and in the ways we serve.

The next question we will explore is Satan's favorite. We will uncover his greatest trick and reveal a secret he uses to destroy your relationships, particularly your relationship with God.

Let's find out what Satan's first question was and how he still uses it today.

CHAPTER TWO

The First Question Ever Asked

What if you met Satan? What would he look like? Cartoons portray him dressed in a red suit and holding a pitchfork. You always know it is him because he has a long tail, horns and looks as if he is on fire. He usually appears silly, stupid and easily defeatable. However, the Bible describes him differently. The Bible says Satan comes in disguise as an angel of light and a servant of righteousness (2 Cor. 11:14-15). This is quite different than the Satan displayed in cartoons.

Satan has a question for you. His question is the first question ever recorded in history. His question is devious, destructive and filled with doubt. His question is the greatest trick in the book.

In Genesis 3:1 we meet Satan for the first time. "Now the serpent was more crafty than any beast of the field which the Lord God had made." Other Bible translations use the word "subtle" or "clever." Satan is devious and scheming. He is crafty, clever and has a subtle plan for you and it is to lie, steal, kill, and destroy your life.

Satan cunningly whispered a question to Eve, initiating a relationship: "Did God really say?" (Gen. 3:1). This is it—Satan's first question and the greatest trick in the book.

"Did God really say?" Satan knows that if you can be tricked into doubting God's Word then you are open to listen to counsel outside of the Bible. This trick insidiously comes in the form of a question.

Using a question to get you to doubt God is a subtle, sinister tactic. It is hard enough not to listen to Satan's questions when you do know God's Word. Yet, it is even harder when you don't remember or don't even know what God said in the first place.

My friend Paul presented a message on how to share the gospel at the University of California Santa Cruz. Paul began his message on evangelism by holding up a copy of *The Satanic Bible* by Anton Lavey, and asked the class, "Does anyone know the main thesis or main premise of this book?"

The class was stunned and so was I.

Paul mentioned that Anton Lavey, the American founder and high priest of the Church of Satan, had lived right down the street in a community called Ben Lomond, California. This made us even more uncomfortable. Everyone was perplexed and did not know how to answer the question. Yet, he asked us again, "Does anyone know the main thesis that Satan wants you to embrace?" He really had me thinking. Perhaps, the main point is to hate God. Nope, that would be too overt. *Maybe it is to lie, steal, and to lust after power, money, and sex.* No, too obvious. I learned that the lie is even more clever than I suspected.

The main premise of *The Satanic Bible* is this: **Do whatever you please.**

Do whatever you please. Very clever. Very devious. Be your own god and submit to no one. Within that command is the opportunity to create a god from your own desires. This command is the embodiment of selfishness, pride and reliance upon self as the source of truth, discernment and understanding. At the core of this is the exaltation of self over God. Jesus taught the exact opposite as He said, "For whoever exalts himself will be humbled, and whoever humbles himself will be exalted" (Matt. 23:12).

Even more devious is the fact that we find this command appealing. Our problem is that we naturally do as we please and are usually pleased by what we do. What we need to learn and train our minds to think is, *How can I do what pleases God?*

Satan will deceive you. It all starts with being distracted from God's Word or perhaps not even knowing what God has written. We are instructed to let the Word of God dwell in us richly (Col. 3:16) so that we can have the Lord direct our footsteps according to His Word (Psalm 119:133). The Bible is our guide for living. Consider this acrostic for the Bible:

B – Basic
I – Instructions
B – Before
L – Leaving
E – Earth

The Bible is our instruction book for relationships, communication and how to obey the Lord who guides us in paths of righteousness for His name's sake (Psalm 23:3).

Satan wants you to listen to his voice, rather than God's. Sadly, many of us fall prey to this trick time and time again.

Combating Satan involves knowing what the Scripture says. As Jesus was tempted by the devil in the desert He continually responded with, "It is written . . . It is written . . . It is written . . ." Jesus Christ gives us His example to follow. Satan knows the Scriptures extraordinarily well. That is why for us, knowing God's Word is imperative to fight spiritual battle so that we "can encourage others by sound doctrine and refute those who oppose it" (Titus 1:9).

How are you doing in this regard? Are you growing in the knowledge of God by studying His book? Consider these passages.

- **Joshua 1:8-9** says, "Do not let this Book of the Law depart from your mouth; meditate on it day and night, so that you may be careful to do everything written in it. Then you will be prosperous and successful."
- **Psalm 1:1-3**, "Blessed is the man who does not walk in the counsel of the wicked or stand in the way of sinners or sit in the seat of mockers. But his delight is in the law of the Lord, and on his law he meditates day and night. He is like a tree planted by streams of water, which yields its fruit in season and whose leaf does not wither. Whatever he does prospers."
- **Psalm 19:7-11** states, "The law of the Lord is perfect, reviving the soul. The statutes of the Lord are trustworthy, making wise the simple. The precepts of the Lord are right, giving joy to the heart. The commands of the Lord are radiant, giving light to the eyes. The fear of the Lord is pure, enduring forever. The ordinances of the Lord are sure and altogether righteous. They are more precious than gold, than much pure gold; they are sweeter than honey, than honey from the comb. By them is your servant warned; in keeping them there is great reward."
- **2 Corinthians 10:4-5**, "The weapons we fight with are not the weapons of the world. On the contrary, they have divine power to demolish strongholds. We demolish arguments and every pretension that sets itself up against the knowledge of God, and we take captive every thought to make it obedient to Christ."

My friend Tom says, "If I can see your schedule and your checkbook, I will know what is really important in your life." Our schedule reveals our habits and where we are investing our time. If you were to meet with your pastor to review your schedule and to show him how much time you dedicate toward reading God's Word and prayer, would you be embarrassed or overjoyed at this meeting?

Consider this: I am your constant companion. I am your greatest helper or your heaviest burden. I will push you onward or drag you down to failure. I am at your command. Half of the tasks that you do you might just as well turn over to me and I will do them quickly and correctly. I am easily managed; you must merely be firm with me. Show me exactly how you want something done; after a few lessons I will do it automatically. I am the servant of all great people and alas of all failures as well. Those who are great I have made great, those who are failures I have made failures. I am not a machine, but will work with all the precision of a machine, plus the intelligence of a person. Now you may run me for profit or you may run me for ruin. It makes no difference to me. Take me, train me, be firm with me, and I will lay the world at your feet. Be easy with me and I will destroy you. Who am I? I am called **Habit**.[9]

There are things we believe and things we think we believe. We act on what we believe. What we believe, we do. If you believe God's Word is important, your habits will reflect this. It is important to understand that you will not win spiritual battles without using God's Word and prayer as your weapons.

Studying the Bible and prayer are two vitally important habits to develop. The payoffs are wisdom, perspective and the joyful intimacy of knowing God. Biblical discipline has value in this present life and the life to come (1 Tim. 4:8). The Apostle Paul writes, "This is a trustworthy saying that deserves full acceptance (and for this we labor and strive), that we have put our hope in the living God, who is the Savior of all men, especially of those who believe" (1 Tim. 4:9-11).

Satan's greatest trick—the greatest trick in the book—is getting you to doubt God's Word. We are directed to let the Word of Christ dwell richly in our heart and mind (Col. 3:16) and to remember, "the one who is in you is greater than the one in the world" (1 John 4:4).

Think of the distractions keeping you from studying your Bible, fellowshipping with believers and taking time to pray. Take a moment and list these distractions. I have been working on a few. Add your distractions below. Write your new action steps to replace the old habits.

Distraction	New Focus	Action Steps
Worldliness and materialism	Focused time in prayer and reading God's Word (John 17:17, Acts 6:4, Col. 3:2, 1 Peter 2:2, 1 John 2:15-17). Living with less while enjoying whatever God provides.	Scheduling time in the morning and while traveling to read my Bible. Keeping a prayer journal to record what and who I am praying for.
Idle conversations	Engaging others with conversations about God and the Scriptures (Deuteronomy 6, Col. 4:5-6, Eph. 6:19-20).	Writing books about God and asking the questions God uses in the Bible with friends, family and people I meet.
Selfishness	Thinking about how to serve others. Godly thoughts and examples of servant-leadership (Phil. 2:3-4; 4:8, Matt. 6:33, Rom. 12:1-2).	Asking, "How can I help?" Sharing resources, study tools and inviting others to Bible studies and prayer groups.
Your Distractions	*New Focus*	*Action Steps*

When someone asks, "Did God really say?" search the Scriptures to find an answer instead of responding with, "I feel . . ." or " I'm not sure . . ." or "I don't know. . ." If you respond with your own thoughts, feelings and words—you risk being deceived and led astray. Satan will have you right where he wants you—listening to his voice and engaged in a relationship with him.

We must train ourselves to listen to the voice of God and trust God's Words. "My sheep listen to my voice; I know them, and they follow me" (John 10:27). Knowing God's voice steers us clear of Satan's tricks and we know God's voice by knowing God's Word. Just like parents recognize their child's voice in a crowd, so you will distinguish God's voice by deepening and developing your relationship with Him through time spent in His book, the Holy Bible.

God's second question to Adam was, "Who told you that you were naked?" In other words, who have you been listening to? Be in tune with God's voice and do not be unaware of Satan's schemes (2 Cor. 2:11).

Here are a few suggestions to help.

- **Go for a walk.** Talk with God. Schedule time for prayer. Think about what is capturing your attention. What things, people or questions are building you up or tearing you down? Ask the Lord to show you the distractions Satan is using in your life. Make a list and attach appropriate Bible passages that will help you implement godly changes.
- **Take an inventory of who you associate with.** Who is influencing your life the most at this moment? Scripture says, "He who walks with the wise grows wise, but a companion of fools suffers harm" (Prov. 13:20). 1 Corinthians 15:33 reminds us, "Do not be misled: Bad company corrupts good character." James 3:13 asks, "Who is wise and understanding among you? Let him show it by his good life, by deeds done in the humility that comes from wisdom." Ask God to bring wise people into your life and seek them out as well.
- **Phone or visit your pastor.** Ask him to help you grow in godliness. The book of James says that if you want to have life at its best, here is what you are to do: "Do not merely listen to the word, and so deceive yourselves. Do what it says. Anyone who listens to the word but does not do what it says is like a man who looks at his face in a mirror and, after looking at himself, goes away and immediately forgets what he looks like. But the man who looks intently into the perfect law that gives freedom, and continues to do this, not forgetting what he has heard, but doing it—he will be blessed in what he does" (James 1:22-25). Join a Bible study. Develop habits in your life that help you recall God's Word and surround yourself with people who share this common goal.
- **Keep a prayer journal.** Write down your prayers and favorite Bible passages to remind you what to focus on. Keep a record of answered prayers and how God has specifically provided, protected and placed people in your life to help.
- **Schedule a time to read your Bible.** Make this a daily habit. Cherish and look forward to this time each day as you grow in the "grace and knowledge of the Lord" (2 Peter 3:18).

One simple word has the power to put you into relationships. Through a question Satan can offer you a relationship based on lies, doubt and despair. God invites you to listen, read and obey His words and this relationship is built on obedience, love and a serving heart.

Ask God to show you the distractions Satan is using in your life. Ask the Lord to help you keep focused on Jesus who is the author and perfecter of your faith. Ask for discernment to quickly recognize the greatest trick in the book packaged in the first question ever asked.

We have examined Jesus' most frequently asked question, *What do you want me to do for you?* and Satan's first question, *Did God really say?* Now we will look at a question you will want to avoid in your relationships with God and with others.

CHAPTER THREE

One Question to Avoid in Relationships

W e can ask another person questions and we can ask God questions. However, there is one question that needs special care and delicate handling. This is one question I would strongly encourage you to avoid in your relationships with God and one another. That one question is the *why* question.

Right about now, you're probably wondering, *Why?*

A why question typically passes judgment. For example, we may ask another, "*Why* were you late?" If their response is not what we deem acceptable, we typically pass judgment and respond with something like, "That's no excuse. You should have arrived on time!" This is where a quarrel usually begins.

Instead of opening with, "*Why* were you late?" how about asking, "*What* is the reason you were late?" Or, "*What* kept you from making it on time?" The answers to these questions allow for deeper understanding and will ellicit more information while steering clear of a judgmental tone.

Be forewarned, if the response to the why question is not sufficient for the person asking, an argument will soon commence. *Why* did you burn my toast? *Why* didn't you listen to me? *Why* are you looking at me like that? *Why* are you wearing that? With these questions one person will probably leave the conversation upset, dismayed, or feeling harshly judged.

Avoiding the *why* question in your relationships will not only help to keep the peace, but will gain the same information you were requesting in the first place, without the drama.

This same principle applies when we communicate with God. How many of us have dropped to our knees or raised our fists and asked God:

Why are you allowing this to happen?
Why don't you help me?
Why won't you respond to my prayers?
Why don't you get me out of this mess?

Sound familiar? At some point in life, when things are not going as planned, we unload the *why* question on God.

As tough as it sounds, from a theological standpoint, God does not have to answer any of our *why* questions. Consider these passages:

- Our God is in heaven; He does whatever pleases Him. Psalm 115:3
- The Lord does whatever pleases Him, in the heavens and on the earth, in the seas and all their depths. Psalm 135:6
- Do not say, "*Why* were the old days better than these?" For it is not wise to ask such questions. Ecclesiastes 7:10
- When times are good, be happy; but when times are bad, consider: God has made the one as well as the other. Ecclesiastes 7:14
- I form the light and create darkness, I bring prosperity and create disaster; I, the LORD, do all these things. Isaiah 45:7

Picture a courtroom where you, the judge, call God to the witness stand and say, "Explain Yourself; *why* are You doing this? I am judging Your behavior and it had better make sense to me." Can you feel the heaviness and judgmental tone of these questions?

What type of people would we be without difficult trials? Trials can bring us to a personal breaking point, and it's that breaking point that brings us to our knees. Until we reach a point where we see God as everything and ourselves as nothing in comparison, we have yet to know God. It is at this point that we begin to depend more on the Lord and less on ourselves.

God allows trials for good reason. One reason is that it strengthens our faith and can result in thankfulness afterwards. 1 Peter 1:6-7 says, "In this you greatly rejoice, though now for a little while you may have had to suffer grief in all kinds of trials. These have come so that your faith—of greater worth than gold, which perishes even though refined by fire—may be proved genuine and may result in praise, glory and honor when Jesus Christ is revealed."

We will experience trouble in this world; the Lord has told us to expect it and not to be surprised by it. But we do not like that our life is hard and some things simply do not make sense. However, we should gain comfort knowing this hard and confusing world is not our home. Here on earth, we are merely vapors and shadows that appear for a little while and then pass away. The Apostle Paul wrote, "Our citizenship is in heaven"

(Phil. 3:20). And in Ecclesiastes, Solomon conveys the truth that we have been created from dust and to the dust we shall return (Ecclesiastes 3:20). The Bible asks, "What is your life? You are a mist that appears for a little while and then vanishes" (James 4:14).

Understanding our true citizenship does not mean we are not allowed to ask questions. In fact, learning to ask God the right questions during times of trial, testing and tribulation can ease some of the frustration during these times. Life is short and in our brief time here we need to learn to communicate with God in times of trouble and seek His help. Asking the right questions during these times can prove beneficial during tough, tough times.

In the Bible, there is a story about a man named Job. We read about Job losing his family, his fortune, and his farm within a matter of moments. After this sudden disaster, the Bible says, "Job got up and tore his robe and shaved his head. Then he fell to the ground in worship and said: Naked I came from my mother's womb and naked I will depart. The Lord gave and the Lord has taken away; may the name of the Lord be praised'" (Job 1:20-21). Next, even more trouble befell Job as Satan afflicted him "with painful sores from the soles of his feet to the top of his head" (Job 2:7). Even worse, his wife said to him, "Are you still holding on to your integrity? Curse God and die!" His response was, "You are speaking like a foolish woman. Shall we accept good from God and not trouble?" (Job 2:9-10).

Indeed, shall we accept only good from God and not trouble? Job had no idea *why* everything he owned was so brutally destroyed. In spite of this, Job praised God. What an amazing response. How have we, in our current time, come to believe that our lives are supposed to be easy, comfortable and void of adversity? The Bible actually teaches the opposite.

- In this world you will have trouble. But take heart! I have overcome the world. John 16:33
- In fact, everyone who wants to live a godly life in Christ Jesus will be persecuted. 2 Timothy 3:12
- Dear friends, do not be surprised at the painful trial you are suffering, as though something strange were happening to you. But rejoice that you participate in the sufferings of Christ, so that you may be overjoyed when his glory is revealed. 1 Peter 4:12-13

- Therefore do not worry about tomorrow, for tomorrow will worry about itself. Each day has enough trouble of its own. Matthew 6:34

After repeated affliction, Job asked God the *why* question. He desperately wanted the Lord to explain Himself. So would I. Listen to the questions from a man in deep agony: "*Why* does the Almighty not set times for judgment? *Why* must those who know him look in vain for such days?" (Job 24:1) Job did not understand what was happening. Job could not grasp the reason for these trials and wanted an explanation.

Remarkably, the Lord never directly answered Job's *why* question. Instead, the Lord replied through a series of questions. As a matter of fact, God responds to Job with sixty-four of His own questions. The Lord begins with:

Who is this that questions Me?
Brace yourself like a man; I will question you and you shall answer Me.
Who is this that darkens my counsel?
Where were you when I laid the earth's foundation?
Tell Me, if you understand how I laid out the dimensions of the world?
- Job 38:2-5

By asking *why*, Job was presuming to know better than God. He was asking God to sit in the defendant's seat in the courtroom. In response, the Lord made it very clear that He was the Creator of all things. Even through this devastating carnage, God was deepening Job's relationship with Him. Theologian Charles Spurgeon wrote about Job's ordeal in the *Pearl of Patience*, "No doubt, in Job's character, the Lord saw certain deficiencies which we cannot see, which he desired to remove, and perhaps he also selected some special qualities which needed to be supplied; and divine love undertook to complete his perfect character."

God is a masterful designer. As a friend of mine likes to say, "The Lord is large and in charge!" God controls the stars, the earth and everything in it (Psalm 24:1). He controls the lightning bolts (Job 38:35), the strength of horses (Job 39:19), the flight of eagles (Job 39:27) and He even knows you so intimately that He has every hair on your head numbered (Matt. 10:30). The Lord knew what was going on in Job's life. And He knows what is currently going on in your life as well. In fact, He is the one who orchestrates your struggles for His own glory and your growth. "And the God of all grace, who called you to His eternal glory in Christ, after you have suffered a little wh ile, will Himself restore you and make you strong, firm and steadfast. To Him be the power for ever and ever. Amen" (1 Peter 5:10-11).

Sometimes we simply do not know what God is doing. But don't be disheartened. In the Gospels, the disciples frequently had no idea what Jesus was doing either, and they were roommates and traveling companions. On one occasion, as Jesus washed their feet He told them, "You do not realize now what I am doing, but later you will understand" (John 13:7). It is okay not to understand what God may be doing in your life. Perhaps later, you will. Then again, perhaps you may not.

Still, our desire to understand the reasons behind God's actions keeps us up at night and inspires our most fervent prayers. What we need to realize is that God has already graciously given us an answer. Physician and counselor Dr. Robert D. Smith wrote, "We can always answer the question *Why?* with Romans 8:28 and 29. We may not have any other answer but we know that at least God is using all circumstances to make us more like Jesus Christ. Being made like Him is so important that the difficulties and trials of illness are worth the pain."[10]

And we know that in all things God works for the good of those who love him, who have been called according to his purpose. For those God foreknew he also predestined to be conformed to the likeness of his Son, that he might be the firstborn among many brothers.
- Romans 8:28-29

God's questions aren't intended to belittle us; they are intended to build us up. His questions are not intended to punish us; they are intended to powerfully remind us who we are talking to. They do stir our mind; yet they should bend our knees while properly addressing the One who created and controls all things.

Now, God is perfectly comfortable utilizing the *why* question in His communication with us. His judgment is perfect and His questions are for our good to help enhance our learning. He is God. He is omniscient. He knows everything. We do not. For instance, watch how marvelously Jesus uses the *why* question as a perfect judge:

- To the crowds listening to His message during the Sermon on the Mount: **Why** do you look at the speck of sawdust in your brother's eye and pay no attention to the plank in your own eye? Matthew 7:3
- To the disciples on the boat during a storm: "He replied, "You of little faith, **why** are you so afraid? Then he got up and rebuked the winds and the waves, and it was completely calm. Matthew 8:26
- To some of the teachers of the Law: "Knowing their thoughts, Jesus said, "**Why** do you entertain evil thoughts in your hearts?" Matthew 9:4
- To Peter after he began to sink while walking on water: "Immediately Jesus reached out his hand and caught him. "You of little faith," he said, '**why** did you doubt?'" Matthew 14:31
- To some Pharisees and teachers of the Law: "Jesus replied, 'And *why* do you break the command of God for the sake of your tradition?'" Matthew 15:3
- To the rich young ruler who asked Jesus, "What good thing must I do to get eternal life?" "**Why** do you ask me about what is good?" Jesus replied. "There is only One who is good. If you want to enter life, obey the commandments." Matthew 19:16-17
- To the Pharisees and Herodians who were trying to set Jesus up: "But Jesus, knowing their evil intent, said, 'You hypocrites, **why** are you trying to trap me?'" Matthew 22:18
- To the indignant disciples after they asked, "**Why** this waste?" as Mary came to Jesus with perfume: "Aware of this, Jesus said to them, '**Why** are you bothering this woman? She has done a beautiful thing to me.'" Matt 26:10
- To His disciples and a great number of people from all over Judea: "**Why** do you call me, 'Lord, Lord,' and do not do what I say?" Luke 6:46

When God uses the *why* question, He already knows the answer. He is the righteous judge, knowing the thoughts and intentions of our hearts (Hebrews 4:12). His judgment is perfect, precise and pure. Ours is not.

Learning from these passages and Job's example, we should be very careful with the *why* question, especially when directed toward God and others. Job later confessed, "I know that you can do all things; no plan of yours can be thwarted. You asked, 'Who is this that obscures my counsel without knowledge?' Surely I spoke of things I did not understand, things too wonderful for me to know. You said, 'Listen now, and I will speak; I will question you, and you shall answer me.' My ears had heard of you but now my eyes have seen you. Therefore I despise myself and repent in dust and ashes" (Job 42:2-4). Job realized that he had misunderstood God's orchestration of all the events happening in his life. He responded with repentance and humility. Job knew God can do all things and shortly after this conversation, "The Lord made him prosperous again and gave him twice as much as he had before" (Job 42:10). We really never know what God is going to do but we do know He can do all things.

On a side note, the *why* question can work when we are simply obtaining information. Any two-year-old uses the *why* question like a machine gun. *Why* is the sky blue? *Why* is the earth round? *Why* is the grass green? *Why* can't I have desert before dinner? However, even at this age, a better question may be formed with a how or what. How did the sky become blue? How does grass become green? What is the reason I can't eat candy all day long? Answers to these questions will elicit more information and steer clear of the judgmental tone.

I invite you to start using more *how* and *what* questions. Avoid asking *why* for one day and see what you learn. Ask the Lord to show you if you are using it in a judgmental fashion. Your conversations will improve and you can obtain better information without passing judgment so quickly.

Avoiding the *why* question develops better relationships with God and others. Jesus said, "For I did not speak of My own accord, but the Father who sent Me commanded Me what to say and how to say it" (John 12:49). Let Jesus have the monopoly on the *why* question.

We have focused on the power of questions and how questions place us into relationships. Jesus' most frequently asked question invites you to have a fulfilling life by being filled with the knowledge and understanding of Him. Satan's first question attacks this relationship and distracts you by challenging what God has said. Avoiding the *why* question will allow you to develop and deepen many relationships while steering clear of a judgmental tone. So much of our life hinges on one simple word. How we **ask** questions and the questions we answer can powerfully impact our lives.

Now, let's explore one question everyone must answer—

CHAPTER FOUR

One Question Everyone Must Answer

In an interview years ago, newscaster David Brinkley asked advice columnist Ann Landers what question she most frequently received from readers. Her answer was, "What's wrong with me?"[11] This is a question we are still asking everyday.

We have scales in our bathrooms. We take personality assessments and constantly look in the mirror to check our hair or makeup. We shower, shave, and clean up nicely. Yet, when our expectations from life do not line up with our reality, many of us are caught asking, *What's wrong with me?*

It can be a debilitating question. The problem is rooted in a constant focus on what I call the unholy trinity of me, myself and I. We are obsessed with ourselves. And, underneath our best efforts to clean up, lurks the problem that we are sinners.

The simple answer to Ms. Landers' question is sin. Sin is what is wrong with all of us because sin separates us from God. Pastor John MacArthur writes in *Man's Biggest Problem* that, "Sin is a destructive thing. This is vividly illustrated in a story told many years ago about Leonardo da Vinci. When Leonardo da Vinci was painting his great masterpiece known as *The Last Supper*, he sought long for a model for Jesus Christ. At last he located a chorister in one of the churches of Rome who was lovely in life and features, a young man named Pietro Bandinelli. Years passed, and the painting was still unfinished. All the disciples had been portrayed except one--Judas Iscariot. After all of those years, da Vinci began the search for a face that had been hardened and distorted by sin...and at last he found a beggar on the streets of Rome with a face so villainous he shuddered when he looked at him. He hired the man to sit for him as he painted the face of Judas on his canvas. When he was about to dismiss the man, he said, 'I have not yet found out your name.' 'I am Pietro Bandinelli,' he replied. 'I also sat for you as your model of Christ.' The sinful years had disfigured the face, and that's the way of sin."[12]

When we sin, we disobey God's commands and this distorts our relationship with Him and others. Over time, our faces can become our own autobiographies; years of living in sin can be as plain as the look on our face. Proverbs 27:19 states, "As water reflects a face, so a man's heart reflects the man." Leonardo da Vinci sure found this to be true in the face of Pietro Bandinelli. Sin affects us physically, emotionally, and, most importantly, spiritually.

The Bible says the payment, penalty and consequence of sin is death (Rom. 6:23). This may seem forward and very direct, but one of only two options will occur when you die. One, you will live eternally with Christ in heaven, which is described as a glorious home with streets of gold, fantastic light, no more tears, pain or sorrow. Or two, you will be eternally separated from Christ and live in eternal torment, darkness and pain in hell. There are no other options.

The question we all need to answer is, "What must I do to inherit eternal life?"

The Bible tells the story of a rich young ruler. I love this story because the man asked the right question, he asked the right person and he asked at the right time. The rich young ruler realized that he longed for something he knew he did not have—eternal life. He also knew Jesus was the only One who could give it to Him.

This rich young ruler went to Jesus and asked, "What must I do to inherit eternal life?" (Mark 10:17). Jesus gave the rich ruler the answer to his question as He looked at him and loved him, "One thing you lack,' He said. 'Go, sell everything you have and give to the poor, and you will have treasure in heaven. Then come, follow me.' At this the man's face fell. He went away sad, because he had great wealth. Jesus looked around and said to His disciples, 'How hard it is for the rich to enter the kingdom of God!'" (Mark 10:21-23). The rich young ruler went away sad. He disregarded God's direct answer to his question. This man chose to "do as he pleased" instead of looking to please the Lord. God really did say to this man, "Go, sell everything you have and give to the poor, and you will have treasure in heaven. Then come, follow me." This confused many who witnessed the encounter. "The disciples were even more amazed, and said to each other, 'Who then can be saved?' Jesus looked at them and said, 'With man this is impossible, but not with God; all things are possible with God'" (Mark 10:26-27).

I think Jesus' offer to the rich young ruler far surpassed any physical possession he could acquire. The riches Jesus offered were packaged in a life of faith and dependence on Him, not in the comforts offered from the possessions and pampering of this world. This rich young ruler met the greatest investment advisor of all-time and didn't heed His counsel. Sadly, he chose his possessions over a personal relationship with the richest person who ever walked the earth.

Now, let's come back to the rich young ruler's question, *What must I do to inherit eternal life?* Have you answered this question personally? Have you ever thought about where you will spend eternity? Are you headed to heaven or hell? If heaven, on what basis will you enter? If hell, how come? And if what you believed were not true, would you want to know the truth? If so, stay with me. If not, be sure you have a biblical answer to the question, *What must I do to inherit eternal life?* Your eternal destination rests upon it.

I would wager $10 that within three questions I could show you that you will not enter heaven based on being good. Would you accept this wager?[13]

Here are the three questions:

Question number one: Have you ever lied? Even a little fib or white lie would count. If so, when someone lies we call them a *liar*.

Question number two: Have you ever stolen something? Even taking a pen from the post office or downloading a licensed computer program without paying for it would be classified as stealing. Taking anything that is not yours is theft. We call this person a *thief*.

Right now, if you answered yes to the aforementioned questions, you have admitted to being a lying thief. If no, are you really telling the truth?

Question number three: Have you ever looked lustfully at a woman? Jesus said "anyone who looks at a woman lustfully has already committed adultery with her in his heart" (Matt 5:28). Jesus' words apply to all of mankind. If you are a woman and have ever looked at a man lustfully then you have committed adultery in your heart as well. Most women actually break the commandment that thou shall not covet more frequently. The commandment of thou shall not covet is certainly broken if you have ever wanted another woman's lifestyle, hairstyle, shoes, purse, or even her figure.

Answering yes to any of these questions is equal to breaking all of God's commandments "for whoever keeps the whole law and yet stumbles at just one point is guilty of breaking all of it" (James 2:10). Under God's justice system, the penalty for breaking just one of His commandments is death (Rom 6:23). *But that is not fair*, you might say. While it may not seem fair, this is God's justice system and we need to conform to His standards.

The Bible says that all liars will have their place in the fiery lake of burning sulfur, which is hell (Rev 21:8). It also says, "Do you not know that the wicked will not inherit the kingdom of God? Do not be deceived: Neither the sexually immoral nor idolaters nor adulterers nor male prostitutes nor homosexual offenders nor thieves nor the greedy nor drunkards nor slanderers nor swindlers will inherit the kingdom of God" (1 Cor 6:9-10).

At this point, ask yourself how are you ever going to enter heaven knowing you have broken God's commands and are sentenced to death in hell? When you realize there is nothing you can do, you will recognize what the rich young ruler never knew—your need for a Savior.

I have lied, stolen and looked lustfully at women. Biblically, that makes me a lying, stealing, adulterer. At the age of seventeen an evangelist shared the bad news and good news from the Bible while I was attending a church in Detroit. The bad news was that sinners are on their way to hell. The good news was that Jesus came to save sinners. For the first time in my life, I realized I was going to hell and asked God for forgiveness of my sins. I repented and God forgave me. All of a sudden life made sense. Jesus is God. The Bible is God's Word and I need to live to please Him above all things. I was born again. This was the greatest news packaged in the greatest story ever told and the greatest day of my life.

Being saved is a gift from God "for it is by grace you have been saved, through faith—and this is not from yourselves, it is the gift of God—not by works, so that no one can boast" (Eph. 2:8-9). When this happens Jesus said, "Then you will know the truth, and the truth will set you free" (John 8:32).

Salvation is found in no one else, for there is no other name under heaven given to men by which we must be saved (Acts 4:12). Jesus said, "I tell you the truth, no one can see the kingdom of God unless he is born again" (John 3:3) and states, "I am the resurrection and the life. He who believes in Me will live, even though he dies; and whoever lives and believes in Me will never die" and then Jesus asks this question, "Do you believe this?" (John 11:26)

Do you believe this?

This question grabs our attention because it points us toward the things that matter the most, namely, our eternal destination and our relationship with Jesus.

Do you see yourself as a sinner in need of a Savior? Do you believe Jesus is the way, the truth, the life, and no one comes to the Father except through Him? (John 14:6) If so, ask to be born again, converted, saved. Ask God to grant you repentance and to have mercy on your soul. Use this one simple word to change your life.

Jesus asked, "What can a man give in exchange for his soul?" The sobering answer is—nothing. A man can give nothing in exchange for his soul and a man profits nothing by gaining the whole world. "For we brought nothing into the world, and we can take nothing out of it" (1 Tim. 6:7). There is only one way someone can be saved from eternal hell and that is through faith in Christ Jesus. Use this one simple word to profoundly impact your life. Ask God to save your soul. Ask.

He saved us, not because of righteous things we have done, but because of His mercy. He saved us through the washing of rebirth and renewal by the Holy Spirit, whom He poured out on us generously through Jesus Christ our Savior, so that, having been justified by His grace, we might become heirs having the hope of eternal life. This is a trustworthy saying. And I want you to stress these things, so that those who have trusted in God may be careful to devote themselves to doing what is good. These things are excellent and profitable for everyone. - Titus 3:5-8

Christ Jesus came to save sinners. Former slave trader and writer of the song Amazing Grace, John Newton said, "I remember two things: that I am a great sinner, and that Christ is a great Savior."[14] And that's why grace is so amazing because we have nothing to offer God in exchange for our soul.

How someone gets saved, becomes converted or born again is beyond my ability to explain. In general, this phenomenal experience occurs by God giving you the gift of eternal life through His Son. 1 John 5:12 says, "He who has the Son has life; he who does not have the Son of God does not have life."

One simple word could change everything—**ask**. Ask to be saved. Ask to be born again. Ask, "What must I do to inherit eternal life?" and embrace God's Word as the greatest authority containing the greatest answer to one of the greatest questions everyone of us must answer.

Closing

What would a world without questions be like? How perplexing would relationships be if you could never ask a question? How long would you want to be with someone who never asked *you* a question?

A world without questions is a world void of curiosity, caring and compassion. In essence, this would be a world without relationships.

Asking is a verb, it is an action and it is a life-changing concept. Humility, wonder, and interest grow stronger as we listen and ask questions. Jesus said, "Ask and it will be given to you; seek and you will find; knock and the door will be opened to you. For everyone who asks receives; he who seeks finds; and to him who knocks, the door will be opened" (Matt 7:7-8).

From the age of twelve we learn Jesus was, "sitting among the teachers listening to them and asking them questions" (Luke 2:46-47). What a great pattern for us to follow.

This skill of asking will allow you to grow personally, professionally and spiritually. This skill will place you in a humble position of continuous learning. This skill will make you more like Jesus.

As Thomas Merton said, "A person is known better by his questions than his answers." Ponder Jesus' words and consider His questions. Discover how a question can reveal assumptions and become the starting point of a discussion. Enjoy exploring, engaging and enriching your relationship with Lord and one another through the application of this one simple word.

Have fun with this knowledge and go tell others about what you are learning.

Go tell others about Jesus' most frequently asked question.
Go tell others about the first question ever asked.
Go tell others about one question to avoid in relationships.
Go tell others about one question we all must answer.
Go tell others about *One Simple Word.*

I will always remember my high school basketball coach's question and I will always remember that questions can profoundly impact our lives. We can ask one another questions. We can ask God questions. And then there are questions God asks us. What will be the questions you'll be remembered for asking?

Ask and watch what a question can do.

Now to Him who is able to do immeasurably more than all we ask or imagine, according to His power that is at work within us, to Him be glory in the church and in Christ Jesus throughout all generations, for ever and ever! Amen.
- Ephesians 3:20

Final Words

The Bible says, "he who refreshes others will himself be refreshed" (Prov. 11:25). If this book has refreshed, rejuvenated or restored a relationship with a friend, family member, or even with God, let me know.

You can send letters through the website at: www.littorch.com.

Also, volume discounts are available to purchase *One Simple Word* for book clubs, small group studies, churches, retreats, and schools. I would be delighted to speak at your church, business, college or conference event. For booking information phone 312.239.8633 or visit the website for details.

LIT TORCH PUBLISHING

www.littorch.com

May your relationship with God be the most precious thing in your life and may He bless you beyond what you could ask or ever imagine—

All the best,

Todd A. Dinulli

P.S. Don't miss the bonus sections. I have included a weekly devotional and over 100+ of Jesus' questions. Furthermore, learn four ways to answer almost any question in the pages ahead.

About The Author

Todd A. Sinelli has served as an advocate and spokesperson for Compassion International and has partnered with Campus Crusade for Christ, Operation Mobilization and various Christian organizations in the United States and abroad.

Todd holds a BBA from Michigan State University, an MBA from the University of Dallas and has studied at The Wharton School's Executive Education Program.

He is a certified biblical counselor through the National Association of Nouthetic Counselors and his current passion is teaching others how to have relationships at their best through the power of one simple word.

Todd has authored three books and enjoys tennis, travel and all things Italian. He resides in Chicago, Illinois and can be contacted through www.littorch.com.

Acknowledgments

Dr. Rick Thomas. Thank you for enlightening and pummeling me with questions. I never knew how much I didn't know until I met you. Your teaching planted many of the seeds in this book that are just beginning to grow and blossom. Thanks for teaching, rebuking, correcting and training me over the years. I look forward to learning even more moves from Batman in the battle to fight the good fight of the faith. Laura Zeender & Jaclyn Zornes. Thank you for your initial help and fastidious attention to detail, ideas, grammar and content. Emanuel & Kelly Balarie. You gave me the format. Todd Martincello. You gave me the perspective. Being in Panama sparked the energy to get serious about this book. Harry Gandia. Loving God is what this is all about. Thank you for sharing your insights and thoughts on how to improve this book. Jim McClarty. Thank you for your words, example and continued perseverance to faithfully teach things of eternal value. I am richer for knowing you. Jim Achilles. Your input, insights and friendship have deeply transformed my understanding of God. From Hollister to Disneyworld, the joy continues to be in the journey. Thank you for helping shape this manuscript and fine-tuning the text. Phil & Laura Clark. Through trips to New York, men's Bible studies and intermittent magic shows, it has been a kick becoming friends with your family and receiving your perspicacious feedback on this book. Rebecca Roundtree. Your prayers, words of encouragement and diligence combing through the edits helped shape this document considerably. Thank you. Duane & Doanie Frederick. Really, my Mensa friends don't think I'm stupid nor do any of them have a duck billed platypus. Thank you for saving me from embarrassing myself by coming alongside and helping with theological integrity, grammar and the correct use of the second person voice. Alyssa Highland. From *The Twig* to *True Riches* to *One Simple Word*, your help has been invaluable. May we be reminded that "urine" for a good time when writing becomes fun and creative. Paul & Jen Legge. You guys have been there from the beginning. Our partnerships in ministry throughout the years have been a kick from days at UCSC to the metropolis of Grass Valley. Thanks for embracing the theme of godliness for 2009. Our best days are yet ahead. May Autumn, Ben, Peter, and Molly rise and call you blessed! Mike & Nanci Perkaus. Prayer and ministry of God's Word—two of the most important things we could be doing. Thank you for continually building me up in these areas. Years have blurred from times at the CBOT to the world of NANC to travels with Compassion. Your friendship has been a major source of blessing in my life. Thank you. Levi, Suzanne, Michele and Tim Nunnink. Thank you for insight and comments on this manuscript. Michele, this book is what happens when you cross John MacArthur with Peter Pan. Tom & Deb Steipp. Thanks for challenging me to include the common thread and to tighten up the text. Lance Murdock. Covers matter. May this book be one you are proud to have on your shelf. Saj & Sheryl Sasi. You provided an amazing sanctuary to refine the core of this book. Thank you in more ways than one. Shoveling snow and babysitting Isabelle and Naveen have been pleasures and great opportunities for me to learn how to become a better servant. May the Lord richly bless you for the grace you've extended toward me. Sharon Durling. Thanks for the continual kick in the pants and persnickety editing. From one author to another, people who write books are nuts. Your best works are yet ahead of you. Keep writing. John Garrison. Thanks for the prayers and continual encouragement to seek first His kingdom. Jeff Sinelli. Thank you for your example to just go for it. In five years, may we both look back and be astonished at what God has done in our lives. All we have to do is keep pushing play. Dad. Thanks for exposing me to the world of education and power of knowledge. You have equipped me with the tools to correctly appraise value. Thank you. Mom. I am glad that of all the moms in this world, the Lord chose you to be mine. Thank you for reading, discussing and giving wonderful feedback throughout the construction of this book. I rise and call you blessed!

Lord Jesus Christ. Without You there is no me. Thank You for giving me perspective and the wonderful privilege of knowing and understanding You. May this book yield everlasting fruit beyond what I could ask or even imagine.

BONUS SECTION 1

Curiosity is Powerful and Attractive

Learning to ask the right questions will deepen and develop your relationships on personal, professional and spiritual levels. By asking questions, you will discover new facets of life, uncover the needs and desires of those near you, and learn details about yourself you might never have known. In short, your life may become full of wonder, awe and discovery. Who knows what fantastic things are in store for you? Perhaps, the only great thing you will gain is a biblical understanding of this one simple word—**ask.**

In the week ahead develop the habit of applying this word. Ask another person to join you for coffee, lunch or dinner and engage in the following exercises. Have fun. Learn. Explore and grow in the grace and knowledge of God (2 Peter 3:18).

MONDAY
Ask God to show you the distractions Satan is using in your life. How are these distractions preventing you from reading your Bible, praying and serving others? Make a list and ask a friend about godly habits both of you could begin implementing.

These three distractions consistently grab my attention:
1.
2
3.

Godly habits that I can replace these distractions with are:
1.
2.
3.

TUESDAY
Do your best to avoid the why question and ask more what and how questions. Keep a record of how many why questions you use throughout the day. Ask the Lord to show you if you are using it in a judgmental manner.

I used the why question _____ times today.

I learned: _____

I should ask more _____ questions.

WEDNESDAY

Have a conversation with a friend, co-worker, fellow student or family member. Invite them to coffee, lunch or for a walk and ask, "What must I do to inherit eternal life?" Listen to their response and then ask, "Where will you spend eternity?" If they do not have a biblical answer, consider reading the chapter *One Question Everyone Must Answer* with them.

A person I would like to ask the question, "What must I do to inherit eternal life?" is: _____ I will invite him / her to join me for coffee / lunch / dinner / or a walk. In this moment, I pray for _____ and ask the Lord to grant them repentance and to save their soul. Lord Jesus, please give me the courage and compassion to engage in this eternally important conversation. Amen.

THURSDAY

Has your relationship with the Lord deepened and developed by reading this book? _____ Specifically, what have you learned about yourself, others and God by exploring how questions can profoundly impact lives?

Can you think of five people who would enjoy reading *One Simple Word*?
1.
2.
3.
4.
5.

Purchase a copy for them or ask them to visit **www.littorch.com** to order their own.

FRIDAY

If Jesus appeared to you personally and asked, "What do you want me to do for you?" What would be your response?

Your response to Jesus' most frequently asked question: _____

Enjoy the following acrostic and may these bonus chapters richly bless your relationship with God and one another beyond what you could ask or even imagine!

Ask God for wisdom (James 1:5, Phil. 1:9-11, Col. 1:9-14).
Seek to help and serve others (Mark 10:45, Phil. 2:4).
Knock down the distractions in your life and replace them with Godly habits (2 Cor. 2:11; 11:14-15).

BONUS SECTION 2

100+ of Jesus' Questions

Jesus' questions from the Gospel of Matthew:

> *Is not life more important than food, and the body more important than clothes? (6:25)*
> *Look at the birds of the air; they do not sow or reap or store away in barns, and yet your heavenly Father feeds them. Are you not much more valuable than they? (6:26)*
> *Who of you by worrying can add a single hour to his life? (6:27)*
> *And why do you worry about clothes? See how the lilies of the field grow. They do not labor or spin. (6:28)*
> *If that is how God clothes the grass of the field, which is here today and tomorrow is thrown into the fire, will he not much more clothe you, O you of little faith? (6:30)*
> *Why do you look at the speck of sawdust in your brother's eye and pay no attention to the plank in your own eye? How can you say to your brother, 'Let me take the speck out of your eye,' when all the time there is a plank in your own eye? (7:3-4)*
> *He replied, "You of little faith, why are you so afraid?" Then he got up and rebuked the winds and the waves, and it was completely calm. (8:26)*
> *Knowing their thoughts, Jesus said, "Why do you entertain evil thoughts in your hearts?" (9:4)*
> *Which is easier: to say, 'Your sins are forgiven,' or to say, 'Get up and walk'? (9:5)*
> *When he had gone indoors, the blind men came to him, and he asked them, "Do you believe that I am able to do this?" "Yes, Lord," they replied. (9:28)*
> *To what can I compare this generation? They are like children sitting in the marketplaces and calling out to others. (11:16)*
> *He said to them, "If any of you has a sheep and it falls into a pit on the Sabbath, will you not take hold of it and lift it out? How much more valuable is a man than a sheep! Therefore it is lawful to do good on the Sabbath." (12:11-12)*
> *If Satan drives out Satan, he is divided against himself. How then can his kingdom stand? (12:26)*
> *"Have you understood all these things?" Jesus asked. "Yes," they replied. (13:51)*
> *Jesus replied, "And why do you break the command of God for the sake of your tradition?" (15:3)*

> *When Jesus came to the region of Caesarea Philippi, he asked his disciples, "Who do people say the Son of Man is?" (16:13)*
> *"But what about you?" he asked. "Who do you say I am?" (16:15)*
> *What good will it be for a man if he gains the whole world, yet forfeits his soul? Or what can a man give in exchange for his soul? (16:26)*
> *"Haven't you read," he replied, "that at the beginning the Creator 'made them male and female,' and said, 'For this reason a man will leave his father and mother and be united to his wife, and the two will become one flesh'?" (19:4-5)*
> *"What is it you want?" he asked. (20:21)*
> *"You don't know what you are asking," Jesus said to them. "Can you drink the cup I am going to drink?" (20:22)*
> *Jesus stopped and called them. "What do you want me to do for you?" he asked. (20:32)*
> *"Do you hear what these children are saying?" they asked him. "Yes," replied Jesus, "have you never read, 'From the lips of children and infants you have ordained praise'?" (21:16)*
> *John's baptism—where did it come from? Was it from heaven, or from men? (21:25)*
> *But Jesus, knowing their evil intent, said, "You hypocrites, why are you trying to trap me?" (22:18)*
> *He asked them, "Whose portrait is this? And whose inscription?" (22:20)*
> *"You snakes! Your brood of vipers! How will you escape being condemned to hell?" (23:33)*
> *Who then is the faithful and wise servant, whom the master has put in charge of the servants in his household to give them their food at the proper time? (24:45)*
> *Aware of this, Jesus said to them, "Why are you bothering this woman? She has done a beautiful thing to me." (26:10)*
> *Then he returned to his disciples and found them sleeping. "Could you men not keep watch with me for one hour?" he asked Peter. (26:40)*
> *Do you think I cannot call on my Father, and he will at once put at my disposal more than twelve legions of angels? But how then would the Scriptures be fulfilled that say it must happen in this way? (26:53-54)*
> *About the ninth hour Jesus cried out in a loud voice, "Eloi, Eloi, lama sabachthani?"—which means, "My God, my God, why have you forsaken me?" (27:46)*

Jesus' questions from the Gospel of Mark:

> *Immediately Jesus knew in his spirit that this was what they were thinking in their hearts, and he said to them, "Why are you thinking these things?" (2:8)*
> *Which is easier: to say to the paralytic, 'Your sins are forgiven,' or to say, 'Get up,*

take your mat and walk? (2:9)

> Then Jesus asked them, "Which is lawful on the Sabbath: to do good or to do evil, to save life or to kill?" But they remained silent. (3:4)

> So Jesus called them and spoke to them in parables: "How can Satan drive out Satan?" (3:23)

> He said to them, "Do you bring in a lamp to put it under a bowl or a bed? Instead, don't you put it on its stand?" (4:21)

> He said to his disciples, "Why are you so afraid? Do you still have no faith?" (4:40)

> "Are you so dull?" he asked. "Don't you see that nothing that enters a man from the outside can make him 'unclean'?" (7:18)

> He sighed deeply and said, "Why does this generation ask for a miraculous sign? I tell you the truth, no sign will be given to it." (8:12)

> He took the blind man by the hand and led him outside the village. When he had spit on the man's eyes and put his hands on him, Jesus asked, "Do you see anything?" (8:23)

> Jesus and his disciples went on to the villages around Caesarea Philippi. On the way he asked them, "Who do people say I am?" (8:27)

> "But what about you?" he asked. "Who do you say I am?" Peter answered, "You are the Christ." (8:29)

> What good is it for a man to gain the whole world, yet forfeit his soul? Or what can a man give in exchange for his soul? (8:36-37)

> They came to Capernaum. When he was in the house, he asked them, "What were you arguing about on the road?" (9:33)

> "What do you want me to do for you?" he asked. (10:36)

> "What do you want me to do for you?" Jesus asked him. The blind man said, "Rabbi, I want to see." (10:51)

> "Should we pay or shouldn't we?" But Jesus knew their hypocrisy. "Why are you trying to trap me?" he asked. "Bring me a denarius and let me look at it." (12:15)

> Jesus replied, "Are you not in error because you do not know the Scriptures or the power of God?" (12:24)

> "Leave her alone," said Jesus. "Why are you bothering her? She has done a beautiful thing to me." (14:6)

> Returning the third time, he said to them, "Are you still sleeping and resting? Enough! The hour has come. Look, the Son of Man is betrayed into the hands of sinners. (14:41)

> "Am I leading a rebellion," said Jesus, "that you have come out with swords and clubs to capture me?" (14:48)

> And at the ninth hour Jesus cried out in a loud voice, "Eloi, Eloi, lama sabachthani?"—which means, "My God, my God, why have you forsaken me? " (15:34)

Jesus' questions from the Gospel of Luke:

> *"Why were you searching for me?" he asked. "Didn't you know I had to be in my Father's house?" (2:49)*
> *Jesus knew what they were thinking and asked, "Why are you thinking these things in your hearts? Which is easier: to say, 'Your sins are forgiven,' or to say, 'Get up and walk?" (5:22-23)*
> *He also told them this parable: "Can a blind man lead a blind man? Will they not both fall into a pit?" (6:39)*
> *Why do you look at the speck of sawdust in your brother's eye and pay no attention to the plank in your own eye? How can you say to your brother, 'Brother, let me take the speck out of your eye,' when you yourself fail to see the plank in your own eye? You hypocrite, first take the plank out of your eye, and then you will see clearly to remove the speck from your brother's eye. (6:41-42)*
> *Why do you call me, 'Lord, Lord,' and do not do what I say? (6:46)*
> *"Where is your faith?" he asked his disciples. In fear and amazement they asked one another, "Who is this? He commands even the winds and the water, and they obey him." (8:25)*
> *"Who touched me?" Jesus asked. When they all denied it, Peter said, "Master, the people are crowding and pressing against you." (8:45)*
> *Once when Jesus was praying in private and his disciples were with him, he asked them, "Who do the crowds say I am?" (9:18)*
> *"But what about you?" he asked. "Who do you say I am?" Peter answered, "The Christ of God." (9:20)*
> *What good is it for a man to gain the whole world, and yet lose or forfeit his very self? (9:25)*
> *"Which of you fathers, if your son asks for a fish, will give him a snake instead? Or if he asks for an egg, will give him a scorpion? If you then, though you are evil, know how to give good gifts to your children, how much more will your Father in heaven give the Holy Spirit to those who ask him!" (11:11-13)*
> *Consider the ravens: They do not sow or reap, they have no storeroom or barn; yet God feeds them. And how much more valuable you are than birds! Who of you by worrying can add a single hour to his life? Since you cannot do this very little thing, why do you worry about the rest? (12:24-26)*
> *If that is how God clothes the grass of the field, which is here today, and tomorrow is thrown into the fire, how much more will he clothe you, O you of little faith! (12:28)*
> *Do you think I came to bring peace on earth? No, I tell you, but division. (12:51)*
> *Then Jesus asked, "What is the kingdom of God like? What shall I compare it to?" (13:18)*
> *"Suppose one of you wants to build a tower. Will he not first sit down and*

estimate the cost to see if he has enough money to complete it?" (14:28)

> Or suppose a king is about to go to war against another king. Will he not first sit down and consider whether he is able with ten thousand men to oppose the one coming against him with twenty thousand? (14:31)

> Suppose one of you has a hundred sheep and loses one of them. Does he not leave the ninety-nine in the open country and go after the lost sheep until he finds it? (15:4)

> Or suppose a woman has ten silver coins and loses one. Does she not light a lamp, sweep the house and search carefully until she finds it? (15:8)

> So if you have not been trustworthy in handling worldly wealth, who will trust you with true riches? (16:11)

> "Suppose one of you had a servant plowing or looking after the sheep. Would he say to the servant when he comes in from the field, 'Come along now and sit down to eat'? Would he not rather say, 'Prepare my supper, get yourself ready and wait on me while I eat and drink; after that you may eat and drink'? Would he thank the servant because he did what he was told to do? So you also, when you have done everything you were told to do, should say, 'We are unworthy servants; we have only done our duty.' " (17:7-10)

> And will not God bring about justice for his chosen ones, who cry out to him day and night? Will he keep putting them off? I tell you, he will see that they get justice, and quickly. However, when the Son of Man comes, will he find faith on the earth? (18:7-8)

> Jesus stopped and ordered the man to be brought to him. When he came near, Jesus asked him, "What do you want me to do for you?" "Lord, I want to see," he replied. (18:40-41)

> For who is greater, the one who is at the table or the one who serves? Is it not the one who is at the table? But I am among you as one who serves. (22:27)

> Then Jesus asked them, "When I sent you without purse, bag or sandals, did you lack anything?" "Nothing," they answered. (22:35)

> He asked them, "What are you discussing together as you walk along?" They stood still, their faces downcast. (24:17)

> "Did not the Christ have to suffer these things and then enter his glory?" (24:26)

> He said to them, "Why are you troubled, and why do doubts rise in your minds?" (24:38)

> And while they still did not believe it because of joy and amazement, he asked them, "Do you have anything here to eat?" (24:41)

Jesus' questions from the Gospel of John:

> "Dear woman, why do you involve me?" Jesus replied, "My time has not yet come." (2:4)

> *"You are Israel's teacher," said Jesus, "and do you not understand these things?" (3:10)*

> *I have spoken to you of earthly things and you do not believe; how then will you believe if I speak of heavenly things? (3:12)*

> *When Jesus saw him lying there and learned that he had been in this condition for a long time, he asked him, "Do you want to get well?" (5:6)*

> *How can you believe if you accept praise from one another, yet make no effort to obtain the praise that comes from the only God? (5:44)*

> *But since you do not believe what he wrote, how are you going to believe what I say? (5:47)*

> *Aware that his disciples were grumbling about this, Jesus said to them, "Does this offend you? What if you see the Son of Man ascend to where he was before!" (6:61-62)*

> *"You do not want to leave too, do you?" Jesus asked the Twelve. (6:67)*

> *Why is my language not clear to you? Because you are unable to hear what I say. (8:43)*

> *Can any of you prove me guilty of sin? If I am telling the truth, why don't you believe me? (8:46)*

> *Jesus said to her, "I am the resurrection and the life. He who believes in me will live, even though he dies; and whoever lives and believes in me will never die. Do you believe this?" (11:25-26)*

> *Then Jesus said, "Did I not tell you that if you believed, you would see the glory of God?" (11:40)*

> *When he had finished washing their feet, he put on his clothes and returned to his place. "Do you understand what I have done for you?" he asked them. (13:12)*

> *Then Jesus answered, "Will you really lay down your life for me? I tell you the truth, before the rooster crows, you will disown me three times! (13:38)*

> *Jesus answered: "Don't you know me, Philip, even after I have been among you such a long time? Anyone who has seen me has seen the Father. How can you say, 'Show us the Father'? Don't you believe that I am in the Father, and that the Father is in me? The words I say to you are not just my own. Rather, it is the Father, living in me, who is doing his work. (14:9-10)*

> *Jesus, knowing all that was going to happen to him, went out and asked them, "Who is it you want?" (18:4)*

> *"Why question me? Ask those who heard me. Surely they know what I said." (18:21)*

> *When they had finished eating, Jesus said to Simon Peter, "Simon son of John, do you truly love me more than these?" "Yes, Lord," he said, "you know that I love you." Jesus said, "Feed my lambs." (21:15)*

> *Jesus answered, "If I want him to remain alive until I return, what is that to you? You must follow me." (21:22)*

BONUS SECTION 3

4 Ways to Answer Most Questions

There are several ways to answer most questions. We will explore four of those options. One response truly honors the person. Two responses slightly honor the person. And the last response not only dishonors the person, but also the request.

For example, suppose someone asks you, *Would you please take out the trash?* One way to answer this question is with complete consent. *Yes, I would be happy to do that for you.* This response honors the person asking. It acknowledges their request and provides an opportunity to serve.

A second way to respond to most questions is through consent with complaint. For example, *Would you take out the trash?* This could be answered, *Yes, but I don't like doing it.* This honors the person while slightly dishonoring the request. The complaint adds nothing to the exchange. Thumper's mother from *Bambi* and my mother used to say, "If you have nothing nice to say, then say nothing at all." Complaining and grumbling really hold no value. The Bible says, "Do everything without complaining or arguing" (Phil 2:14). Let's follow Thumper, mom, and most importantly, God's Word in our service to one another.

A third way to respond is through consent with condition. The question, *Would you take out the trash?* The response given here is, *Yes, I will take out the trash if you clean my car.* Again, this slightly dishonors the request and we can miss the opportunity to serve from a pure motive. We need to learn to consider another's needs above our own. By attaching a condition, we diminish the request and turn the discussion into a negotiation.

Giving complete consent is honorable. Consent with complaint and consent with condition are less honorable responses.

The fourth way to respond to most questions is through the silent treatment. Not responding. Not acknowledging. Not saying a word. *Would you take out the trash?. . . Todd, did you hear me? . . . Todd. . .Todd . . . Toooddddd . . . Would you pleeeeease take out the trash! TODD!* Not saying a word when you hear the person is very dishonoring.

Of course you could always answer, "No" to any question but that response would take a whole different book to explain!

God's Word allows us to become masterful communicators. Romans 15:4 says, "For everything that was written in the past was written to teach us, so that through endurance and the encouragement of the Scriptures we might have hope."

Consider these examples from the Bible of the four ways to respond to most questions:

Responding with **complete consent** as Jesus calls His disciples:

*As Jesus was walking beside the Sea of Galilee, he saw two brothers, Simon called Peter and his brother Andrew. They were casting a net into the lake, for they were fishermen. "Come, follow me," Jesus said, "and I will make you fishers of men." **At once they left their nets and followed him.***
- Matthew 4:18-20

Responding with **complaint:**

Any command God asks us to do should be done without complaining.

*Do everything without **complaining** or arguing, so that you may become blameless and pure, children of God without fault in a crooked and depraved generation, in which you shine like stars in the universe as you hold out the word of life—*
- Philippians 2:14-16

Responding with **condition:**

*As they were walking along the road, a man said to him, "I will follow you wherever you go." Jesus replied, "Foxes have holes and birds of the air have nests, but the Son of Man has no place to lay his head." He said to another man, "Follow me." **But the man replied, "Lord, first let me go and bury my father."** Jesus said to him, "Let the dead bury their own dead, but you go and proclaim the kingdom of God." **Still another said, "I will follow you, Lord; but first let me go back and say good-by to my family."** Jesus*

replied, "No one who puts his hand to the plow and looks back is fit for service in the kingdom of God."
- Luke 9:57-62

Dishonoring response with **silence** from rich young ruler:

*Now a man came up to Jesus and asked, "Teacher, what good thing must I do to get eternal life?" "Why do you ask me about what is good?" Jesus replied. "There is only One who is good. If you want to enter life, obey the command-ments." "Which ones?" the man inquired. Jesus replied, "Do not murder, do not commit adultery, do not steal, do not give false testimony, honor your fa-ther and mother,' and 'love your neighbor as yourself.' " "All these I have kept," the young man said. "What do I still lack?" Jesus answered, "If you want to be perfect, go, sell your possessions and give to the poor, and you will have treasure in heaven. Then come, follow me." **When the young man heard this, he went away sad, because he had great wealth.***
- Matthew 19:16-22

You are now equipped with some valuable tools to enhance your relationships with God and with others. May the use of this one simple word profoundly impact your life in the days ahead—

Endnotes

[1] John Dear, *The Questions of Jesus*, (New York, NY: Doubleday, 2004), 9-10.

[2] Ravi Zacharias, *The Questions of a Man in Agony* (Part 1 of 2), July 3, 2007.

[3] Tom J. Cowley, *A Biography of Jesus* (Tiburon, CA: Eagle's Nest Press, 2005), 36.

[4] S.M. Lockridge, *That's My King!*, http://en.wikipedia.org/wiki/S, 1976.

[5] John Dear, *The Questions of Jesus*, (New York, NY: Doubleday, 2004), 2.

[6] *Rolling Stone Magazine*, Vol. 824, October 28, 1999.

[7] S. Truett Cathy, *Corporate Purpose of Chick-fil-A*, http://www.chickfila.com/?#faqs

[8] The Barna Group, *Survey Details Current Vision of the American Dream*, June 23, 2008.

[9] Dave Ramsey, *Financial Peace*, (New York, NY: Penguin Books, 1997), 30-31.

[10] Rick Thomas, *Theological Framework for Counseling* (Brookfield, IL, Mt. Carmel Ministries, 2004)

[11] John Maxwell, *Attitude 101* (Nashville, TN: Thomas Nelson, 2003), 71.

[12] John MacArththur, *Man's Biggest Problem*, http://www.biblebb.com/files/MAC/sg2217.htm.

[13] Ray Comfort, *Revival's Golden Key: Unlocking the Door to Revival* (Gainesville, FL: Bridge-Logos Publishers, 2002), 211-212.

[14] Chris Tiegreen, *One Year Walk with God Devotional* (Wheaton, IL: Tyndale House, 2004), September 25.

To order additional copies of *One Simple Word* visit

LIT TORCH PUBLISHING

www.littorch.com

Discounts available for large orders.